PAUL JACKSON

Flying Mobiles

Illustrations:
Scoular Anderson

ANGUS
& ROBERTSON
PUBLISHERS

Introduction

Mobiles are cheap, easy to make and great fun! They seem to balance magically in the air, which is why all the models in the book are of things you can see in the sky or out in space.

You can hang each model on its own, or you can make a mobile with several of the same model, such as a squadron of Bi-planes or a flock of Birds. Another idea is to mix models in themes such as a night sky (Man in the Moon, Stars and Planets) or creatures (Birds, Butterflies and Bats). Or you can just put together a group of your favourites.

Most of the models – once assembled – can be collapsed flat, so you can send them to friends as presents. The Star, for example, would be terrific to give as a Christmas present. For birthdays, the trick is to find the right model for the right person.

Mobiles are best hung in moving air, perhaps near a window or door, or even above your bed where the rising warm air from your body will make the models spin. Carefully made, your mobile will be a spectacular spinning sculpture that will amaze everyone.

Please read the next few pages. They explain some of the simple things you will need to know to complete your mobile. Remember to make the models slowly and carefully. The drawings in the Construction section of each model are all to scale. You can decide how big – or small – to make each model, but make sure that when you are asked to measure something, such as the length of a slit, you do it accurately.

Equipment

Card

Use thin card for all the models.

The easiest and cheapest way to collect it is to keep empty breakfast cereal or chocolate boxes, frozen food packets and so on. Old birthday and Christmas cards are also worth keeping, as are stiff covers from glossy magazines and even old LP record covers. Once you start to look, you will be surprised how much card you will find. Ask friends and relatives to collect it for you.

After making some of the projects with these cards, you will want to buy a few big sheets of proper thin card to make some superb finished models. You can buy this card in many beautiful colours from art and craft shops. A big sheet will make about four or five models – enough for a mobile.

Do not use very thick card or cardboard, such as the brown corrugated card used to make large boxes, unless you want to make really **huge** models (have a go!).

Paper of any kind is too thin and floppy for making models, but it is useful for decorating them. You can cut out interesting shapes and patterns from photographs or drawings in magazines, then glue them to the card to make a colourful collage. Or try using shiny kitchen foil, or glitter, or make patterns with packets of gummed paper circles and stars. In fact, if you want to decorate a project ... anything goes! If you have an idea, try it.

If you don't want to decorate anything, the models will still look terrific if you make them in a good card and leave them plain.

Felt Pens and Paint

You can decorate the card with thick coloured felt pens or, for larger surfaces, poster or powder paint. Be careful with the paints though – the water can make some cards 'cockle' or go crinkly. Felt pens are kinder to card.

Scissors and Craft Knife

Cut the card with scissors to make the outline shapes.

The slits through which the different pieces of card slot together, and the shapes which are cut out in the card – like the windows in the Helicopter – have to be made with a craft knife. A craft knife can be dangerous if used carelessly. Always hold it firmly with one hand and put your other hand safely behind the blade, so that it won't cut you if it slips. If you don't want to use a craft knife, ask an adult to use it for you.

Cutting Surface

A craft knife will cut not only through the card, but also through the surface beneath it, so be careful where you use it. Cut on to a large sheet of thick card, hardboard, the back of a sketch pad, or another surface nobody minds being used. Ask first.

You will also need:

Pencils

for drawing out the shapes on the card.

Rubber

for rubbing out mistakes and cleaning off old pencil marks on a finished model.

Ruler

for measuring slits and tabs.

Pair of Compasses

for drawing circles.

The Slot Lock

*This very simple lock is only used a few times in the book – for example, when locking the wings to the fuselage in the Jet – but you need to know how to make it, so practice the example here before starting a model. The important part of the lock is the little slit at **C**. Don't forget it!*

1.

*With a ruler, measure the widest part across a piece of scrap card, here shown in white. On another scrap piece, here shown shaded, draw a line between **A** and **B,** exactly the same length as you have just measured. Use a craft knife and make a slit along the line. Make a small slit at **C** at the point where you want the white card to lock with the shaded piece. Slide the white card through the slit in the shaded piece.*

2.

*Push the white piece to the right, so that **A** goes into the small slit at **C**.*

3.

The Slot Lock complete.

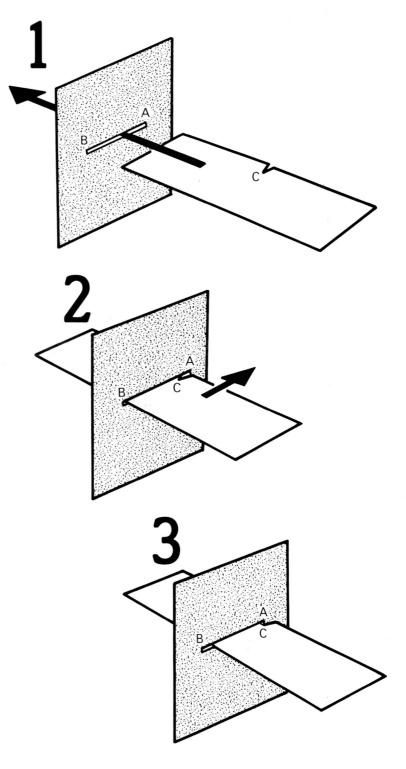

The Bar Lock

This is a very clever lock and very strong. It is used in every model but in slightly different ways each time – look, for example, at the variations in the Star, Helicopter and Butterfly. Make the three examples described here and look out for them in the models – you won't be able to make very much unless you can make a good Bar Lock!

1.

With a craft knife or scissors, make two cuts at one end of a piece of scrap card. Fold in the ends.

2.

Place the card on to another scrap piece (here shaded). With a pencil, make a dot on the shaded piece at the end of each cut.

3.

Make a slit in the shaded piece exactly between the two dots. Hold the shaded piece upright and push the folded tabs of the other piece right through the slit.

4.

Open out the tabs.

5.

The Bar Lock complete.

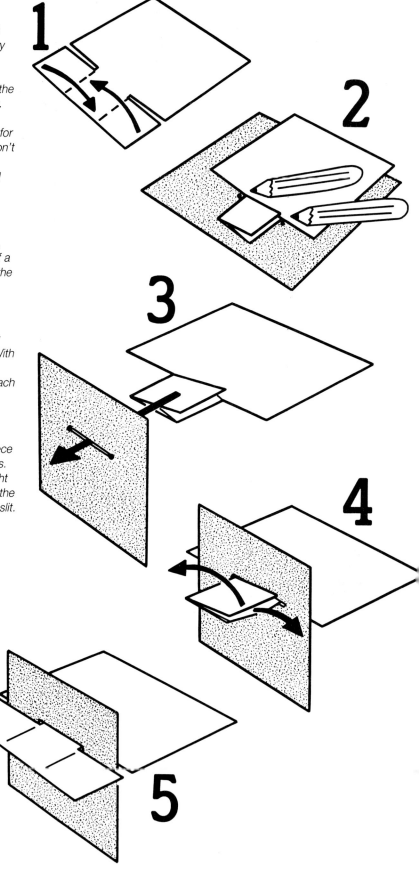

6.

Sometimes, the white piece can have a bar at each end, as here. The card is shaped like a letter H. This shape is used to lock the Hang Glider bars and the Bi-plane struts, amongst other things.

7.

*Sometimes too, the H shape passes through just a single piece, like the wheels on the Bi-plane, the legs on the Bird or the eyes on the Man in the Moon. A clever addition to make the lock even stronger is to cut a small slit at one end of the central fold, rather like the slit at **C** in the Slot Lock.*

How to Suspend a Model

A few models – the Rocket, Planet, Star, Man in the Moon and the Balloon, can be suspended from a single thread of cotton. This is simple enough. The others though, need to be suspended from three threads so that they can balance. The example described here uses a simple Slot Lock shape of card, but the models themselves are sometimes slightly different shapes.

1.

*Thread a needle with a length of cotton. Push the needle through a piece of card from below at **A**, which is some distance from the centre of the model.*

2.

*Go to the opposite side and push the needle back through at **B**, which is the same distance from the centre of the model as **A**. Tie a big knot at **A** so that the cotton cannot slip through.*

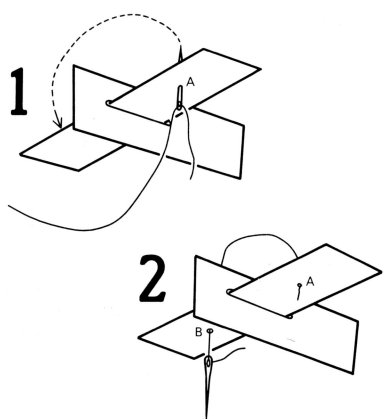

3.

Tie a big knot at **B**, leaving a semi-circle of cotton between **A** and **B**.
Tie a long length of cotton to this semi-circle, with a simple overhand knot. Pull the knot tight.

4.

Push the needle through the far end of the card at **D**.

5.

Tie off the end at **D**.

6A.

The length of cotton between **C** and **D** is important because it can alter the angle at which the model hangs. Here, **CD** is a long length, so that **D** drops low.

6B.

Here **CD** is shorter, so that **D** is level.

6C.

Here **CD** is shorter still, so that **D** is lifted up. Be careful to make **CD** the length you want it to be!

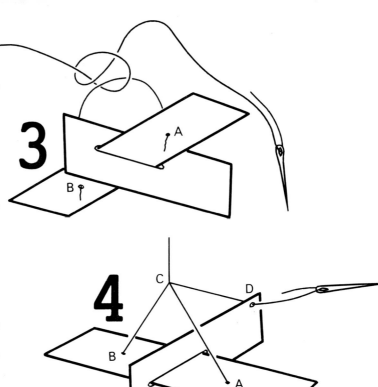

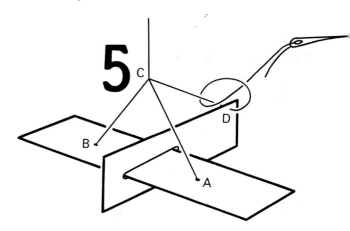

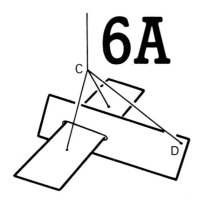

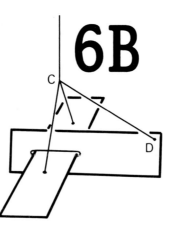

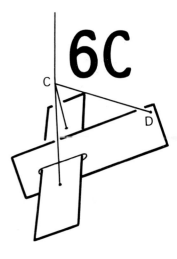

How to Make a Mobile

1.

A model can be hung up all by itself, or with lots of others on separate strings near by. Each will spin round on its own, but the whole group won't spin like a mobile.

2.

To make a mobile like this basic example, you will need a strong horizontal bar. Special mobile wires can be bought in most craft shops, or you can buy florists' wires which are used to make artificial flowers, from flower shops. If you can't find any suitable wire, use thin canes, plastic straws or fire lighting spills.
Always make a mobile from the bottom up. Tie the threads from two models to either end of the wire, straw, or whatever your bar is. Tie another thread to the middle of the bar and slide it to and fro along the bar until it balances.

3.

To make this more complicated mobile, make two simple mobiles as described above, then tie the middle threads to either end of a longer bar. Tie a thread to the middle of the longer bar and balance as before.

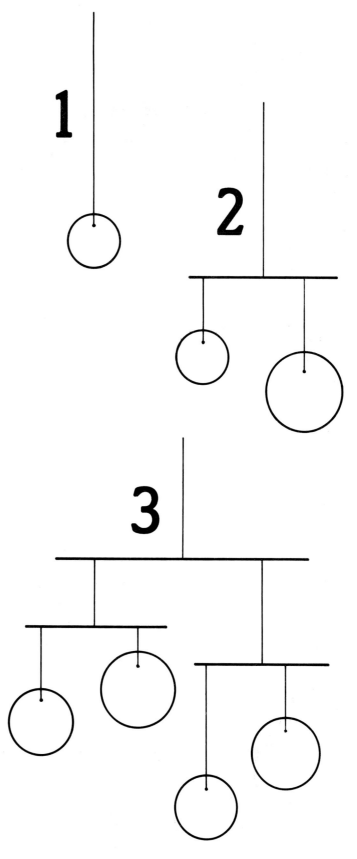

4.

This mobile is simpler than the previous one because one half is just a single model suspended from the top bar, not two suspended from a small bar. It is possible to make very complex mobiles, hanging doubles or singles in many patterns, rather like drawing a family tree going back through the generations. Invent your own! Always make sure that every model can spin through a complete circle without hitting another model, wire or thread.

5.

This is a different idea for a mobile, joining bars in an X shape. It can be used in combination with singles or doubles if you want to make a complicated mobile.

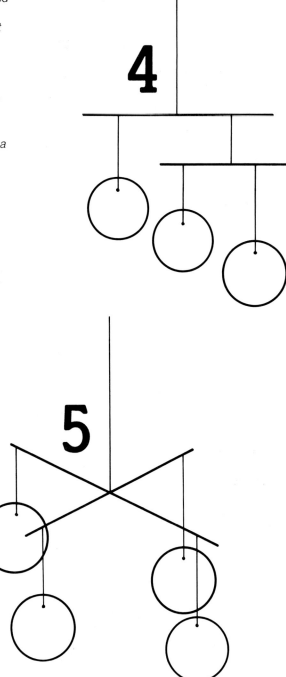

Man in the Moon

The Moon is our nearest neighbour, some 250,000 miles (380,000 km) from the Earth. The smiling face we sometimes see is caused by craters casting dark shadows on the brightly lit surface. Can you remember the name of the first man **on** the Moon? It was Neil Armstrong in 1969.

1

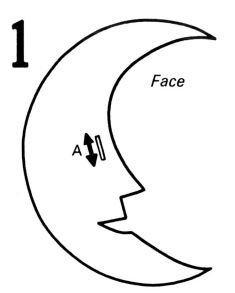

Face

Eyes

2

Construction

1.
Cut out the face. Make a small slit at **A**.

2.
Fold a small piece of card in half. Measure the **A** slit and mark the same length along the crease.
Draw an eye, with crease **A** at one edge, as shown.
Cut it out through both layers (but don't cut along the crease!).
Then cut out or draw a small circle in the middle to make a hole in each eye.

Assembly

A.
Unfold the eyes and fold one over . . .

B.
. . . like this.

C.
Push the folded eye through the slit in the face.

D.
Unfold the eye. This will lock the eyes in the face.

E. *The Man in the Moon complete. Hang the model from a length of thread.*

F.
You can make the face look upwards if you fasten the thread to the top of the card. To make him look down, fasten it near the eye.

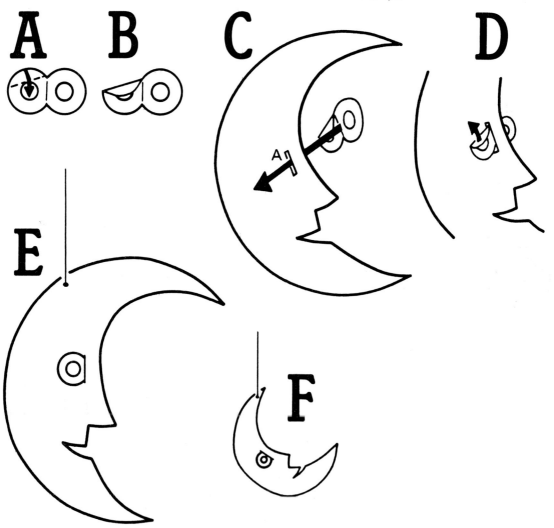

Planet

There are at least nine planets that circle the Sun, and our Earth is one of them. The Earth goes around the Sun once a year, but the outermost planet – Pluto – goes around only once every 248 Earth years. The most beautiful planet is Saturn, famous for its rings which are made of ice and dust.

Construction

1.
Fold a piece of card in half. With a pair of compasses or something circular like a jamjar lid, cup, or roll of tape, draw a circle. Cut it out through both layers of card to make two identical circles.
Make two small cuts at opposite ends of the circles, cutting through both layers. Measure **A**, the distance between the ends of the cuts.

2.
Cut out a circle larger than the first two, and then cut out a circle inside to make a ring. The width of the inner circle **A** should measure the same as **A** in Step **1.**

3.
On one of the two circles (X) make a slit **B** down the middle.

4.
On the other circle (Y), make two cuts on the centre line, so that the gap between them is as long as slit **B**.

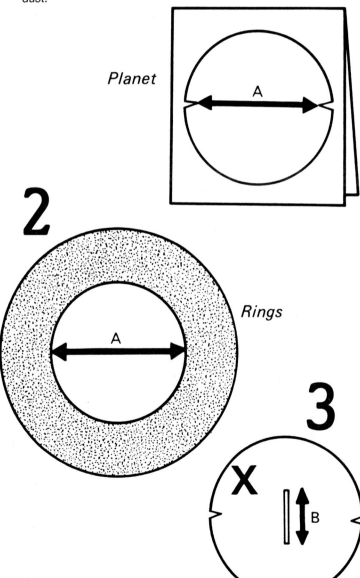

Planet

Rings

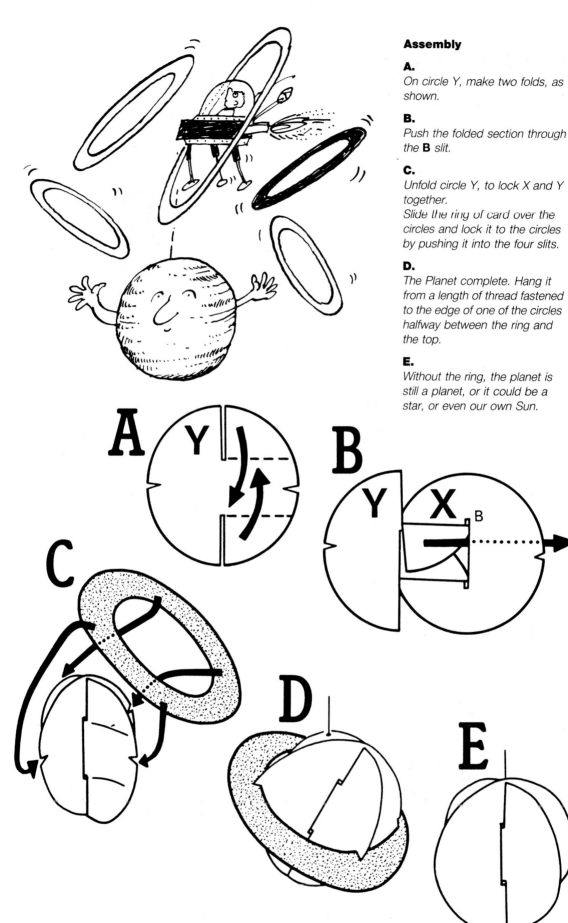

Assembly

A.

On circle Y, make two folds, as shown.

B.

Push the folded section through the B slit.

C.

Unfold circle Y, to lock X and Y together.
Slide the ring of card over the circles and lock it to the circles by pushing it into the four slits.

D.

The Planet complete. Hang it from a length of thread fastened to the edge of one of the circles halfway between the ring and the top.

E.

Without the ring, the planet is still a planet, or it could be a star, or even our own Sun.

Star

The brightest star and the nearest is our Sun. Now some incredible numbers: it is 98,000,000 miles (160,000,000 km) away from the Earth and the next nearest star is 24,800,000,000 miles (40,000,000,000,000 km) away … and that's a long, long, long way! 1,000,000 Earths could fit inside the Sun and its temperature is 15,000,000°C at its centre.

Construction

1.
Fold a piece of card in half. Draw a star shape, then cut it out through both layers to make two identical stars.

2.
On one star shape (X) make slit **A** down the middle.

3.
On the other star shape (Y) make two cuts, so that the gap between them is as long as slit **A**.

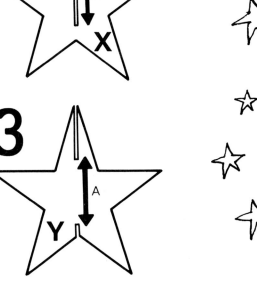

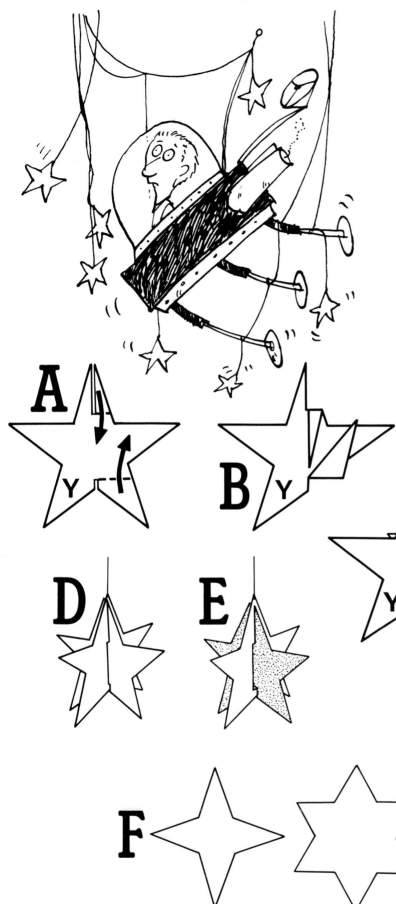

Assembly

A.
On star Y, fold in two of the points, as shown ...

B.
... like this.

C.
Push the folded section through the **A** slit.

D.
Unfold star Y to lock X and Y together. The Star is complete. Hang it from a length of thread.

E.
Try making the Star from two different kinds of card. When it spins, you will see the colours or patterns changing.

F.
Make different Stars with four, six, or even twelve points, as shown here. Don't forget to make two of each!

Rocket

The first rocket to orbit the Earth was the Russian Sputnik satellite, launched in 1957. Since then, hundreds of satellites have been launched. Many men and women have flown in space, and some have even landed on the Moon. In the future, will people live on other planets and never visit the Earth? What will their rockets look like? Invent your own for a mobile.

Construction

1.
Cut out the rocket shape. Make a small slit down the middle at **A** and another across the middle at **B**, as shown.

2.
Fold a piece of card in half. Measure slit **A** and mark the same length along the crease. Draw a leg as wide as **A**. Repeat further along the crease. Cut out each leg through both layers (but not along the crease), to make two pairs of legs.

3.
Draw the afterburn on a single piece of card. Measure slit **B** and make the narrowest part of the flame measure the same distance. Cut out.

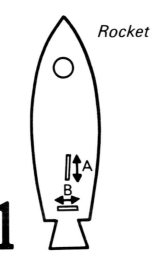

Rocket

1

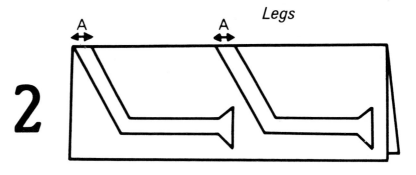

Legs

2

Afterburn

3

Assembly

A.
Make two folds at the end of one foot on each pair of feet.

B.
Fold in the tabs at the top of the T-shape of the afterburn.

C.
Push the narrow foot on each pair of legs through the slit at **A**. Once they are through, unfold them.
Push the top of the afterburn through the slit at **B**, then open out the T-shape to lock it to the rocket.

D.
The Rocket complete. Hang it from a thread fastened halfway down the fuselage.

E.
Try making different rockets, such as this one, or others you've seen in comics, books or films.

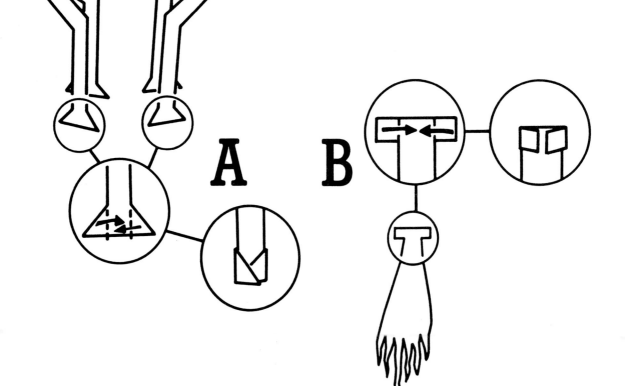

A   B

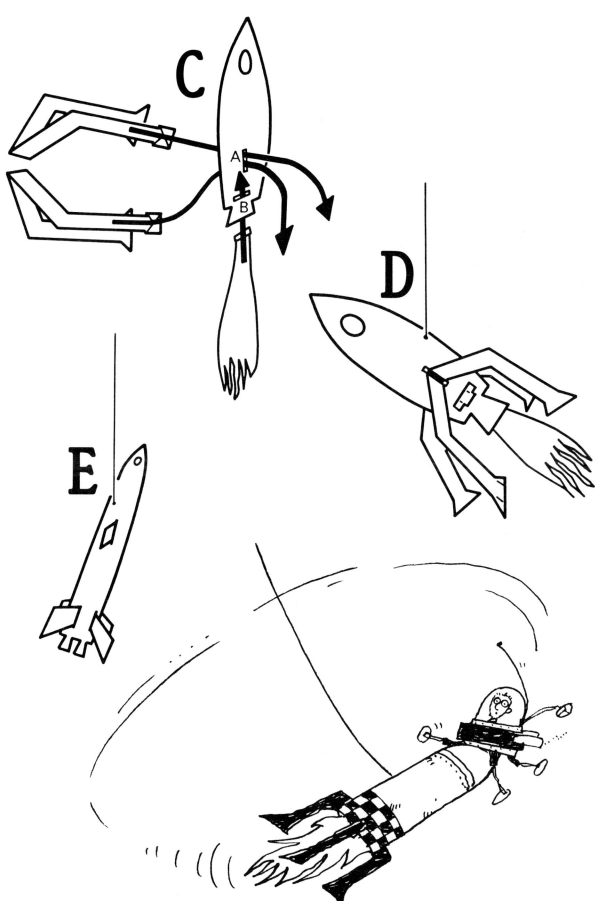

C

D

E

Airship

The age of the airship was in the 1920s and 30s, when huge German Zeppelins regularly carried 200 people across the Atlantic. In those times, the balloons were filled with highly inflammable hydrogen gas. A few tragic crashes brought that elegant era to an end. Today, helium, an inert gas which is completely safe, is used instead of hydrogen and airships are flying again. Have you seen one?

Construction

1.
Fold a piece of card in half. Draw the shape of an airship, then cut it out through both layers to make two identical shapes. On one piece only, make two very small cuts at **A**. Measure distance **B** between them.

2.
Fold a small piece of card in half. Draw the shape of a propeller, then cut it out through both layers to make two identical shapes.

3.
Draw the shape of a cabin, cutting out two windows. Include two T-shapes at the top, which are the distance **B** apart. Measure the **A** slits and make the narrow part of each T the same width. Make small slit **C** at the back of the cabin.

4.
On the airship shape without the **A** slits (shape X), make slit **D** across the middle.

5.
On the other shape (Y), make two slits so that the gap between them is as long as slit **D**.

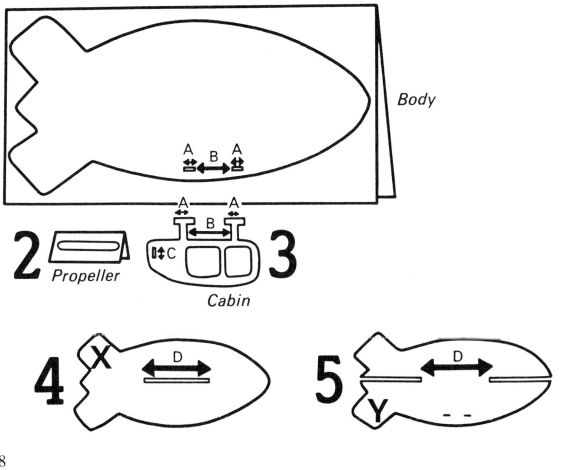

Body

Propeller

Cabin

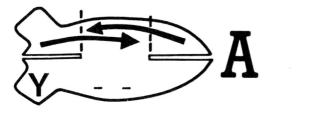

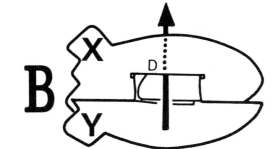

Assembly

A.
On shape Y, make two folds, as shown.

B.
*Push the folded section through slit **D**.*

C.
Unfold Y, to lock X and Y together.

D.
Fold in the tabs at the top of the two T-shapes on the cabin.

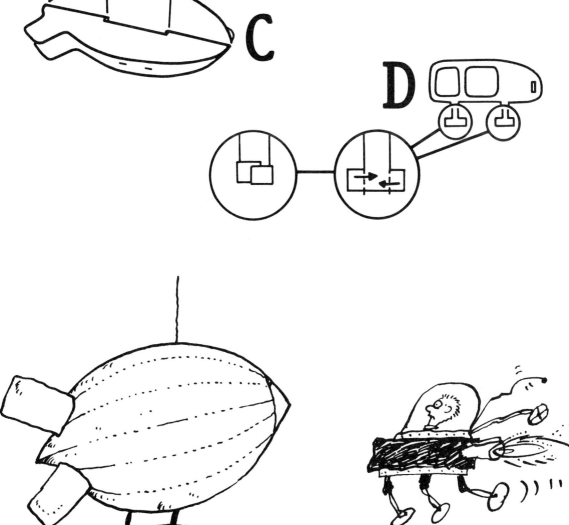

E.
Push them through the slits at **A**, *so that one goes through from the front and the other from the back. This will make the cabin hang in line with the vertical airship shape. Open out the Ts to lock the cabin to the ship.*
Push the propeller blades through the slit at **C**.

F.
The Airship complete. Hang it from a single length of thread, as shown, or from three threads.

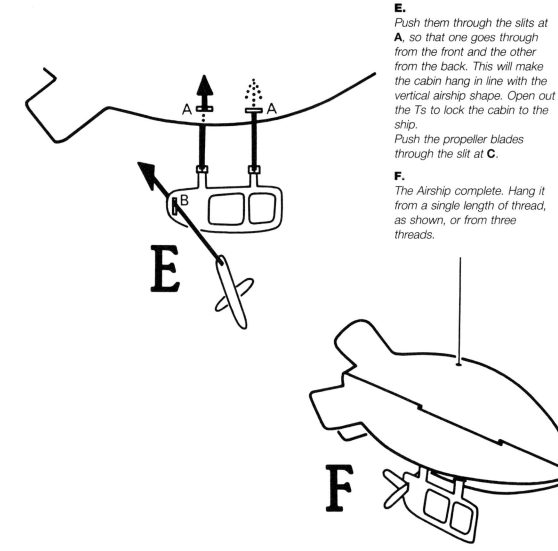

Helicopter

Helicopters are perhaps the strangest of all powered aircraft. They can take off and land in a very small area, they can hover in one place, fly backwards, round in circles – even sideways! Their amazing manoeuvrability makes them ideal for all types of rescue on land and at sea. The largest helicopter has rotor blades a massive 219 ft (67 m) long.

Construction

1.
Cut out the shape of the fuselage. Cut out two windows. Make small slits at **A** and **B** and make a cut into the back edge of the tailplane.

2.
Fold a piece of card in half. Draw a long upside-down T-shape. The narrow part (**B**) should be the same width as slit **B**. Cut out the shape through both layers (but don't cut along the crease).

3.
Fold a piece of card in half. Draw a skid. Make a slit at **B** through both layers, which is the same length as the previous slit **B**. Cut out the shape through both layers to make two identical skids.

4.
Fold a long piece of card in half. Draw a rotor blade and cut it out through both layers to make two identical blades.

5.
Fold a small piece of card in half. Draw a tail rotor blade and cut it out through both layers to make two identical blades.

6.
Cut out the tail wing. Make a cut into the front edge and a small slit at **C**.

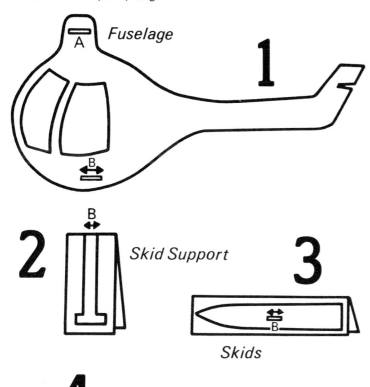

1 Fuselage

2 Skid Support

3 Skids

4 Rotor Blades

5 Tail Rotor

6 Tail Wing

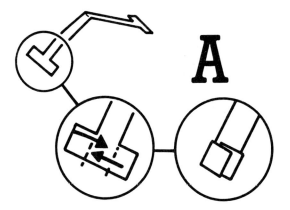

A

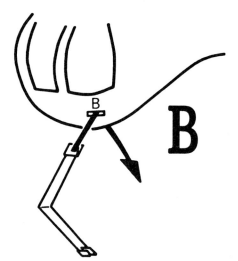

B

Assembly

A.
Make two folds in the ends of the skid supports.

B.
Push one end through the **B** slit in the fuselage and fold the support at the centre.

C.
Push the ends of the skid supports down through the **B** slits in the skids, then unfold the T-shapes to lock the supports to the skids.
Push the rotor blades through the **A** slit. Push the tail rotor blades through the **C** slit, then slot the tail wing into the back of the fuselage.

D.
The Helicopter complete. Hang it from three threads.

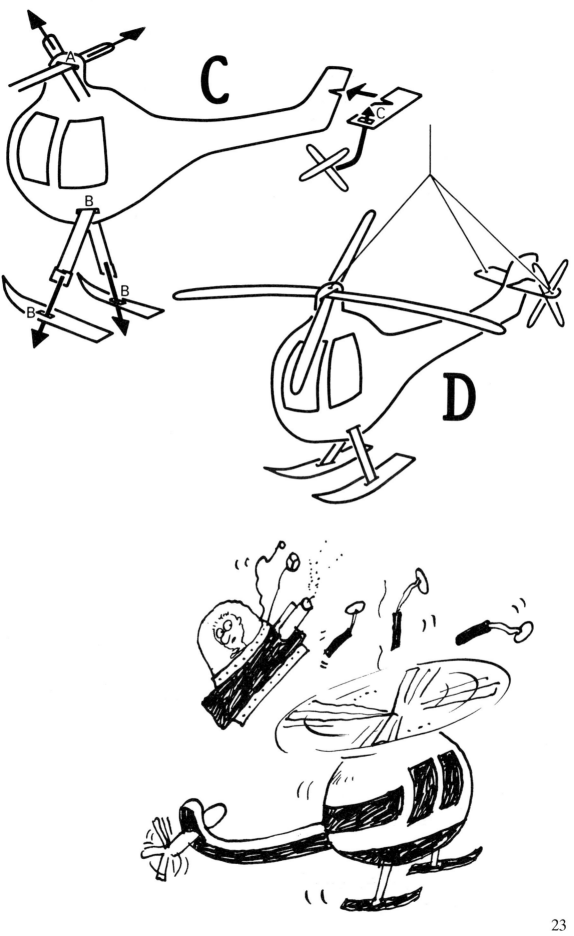

C

D

Jet

A jet engine is a very complicated machine based on a very simple idea: it sucks in air at the front, then squirts it out at the back very fast, pushing the plane forward. Some military jets can fly at 2500 mph (4000 kph), or fly from London to New York in just over an hour.

Construction

1.
Cut out the shape of the fuselage. Make a slit at **A**. Make a cut into the back edge of the tailplane.

2.
Fold a large piece of card in half. Measure a length **A** along the crease, the same size as slit **A**. Draw the wing, as shown. Cut a small slit at **B**, through both layers. Cut out the wing, cutting through both layers but not along the crease.

3.
Fold a small piece of card in half. Away from the crease, draw the shape of a bomb, so that the narrow part of the T-shape on top (**B**) is the same width as slit **B**. Cut out through both layers to make two identical bombs.

4.
Cut out a tail wing with a cut into the front edge.

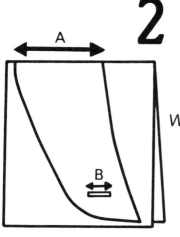

Fuselage

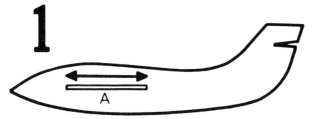

Wings

Bombs

Tail Wing

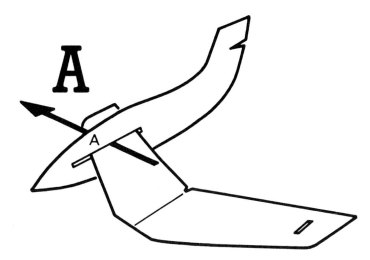

Assembly

A.

*Unfold the wings and push them through slit **A**.*

B.

Fold in the tabs at the top of the T-shapes on the bombs.

C.

*Push the folded sections of the bombs up through the **B** slits, then unfold the T-shapes to lock them to the wings (this is a Bar Lock).*
Slot together the tail wing and the tailplane.

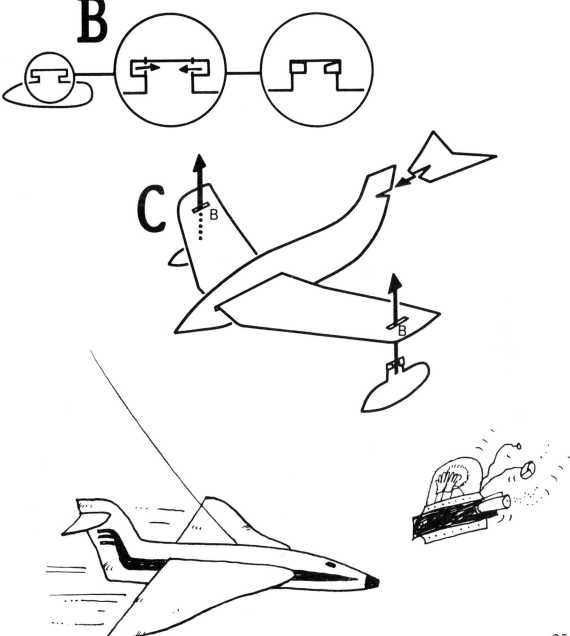

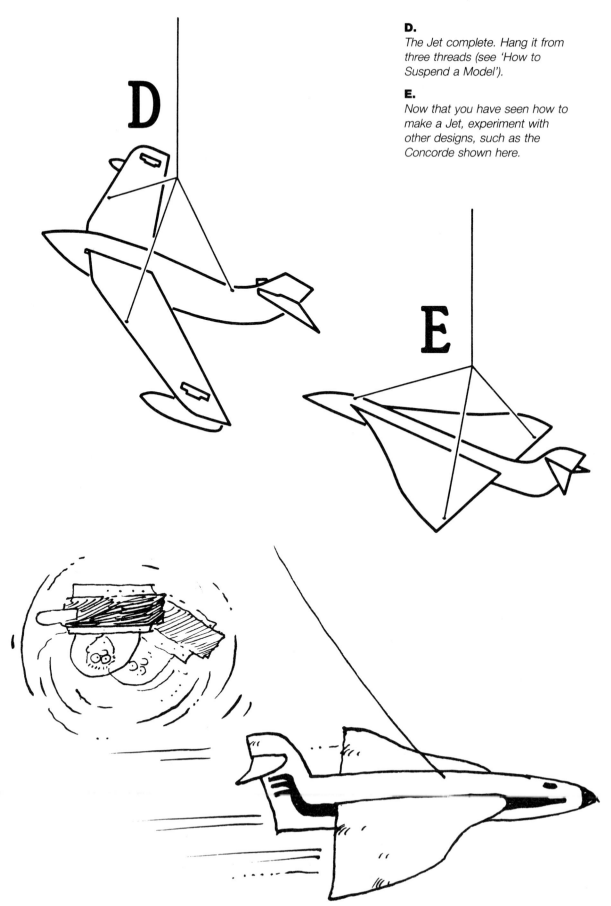

D.

The Jet complete. Hang it from three threads (see 'How to Suspend a Model').

E.

Now that you have seen how to make a Jet, experiment with other designs, such as the Concorde shown here.

Bi-plane

The first aeroplanes to fly were bi-planes. They are very strong, which is why many of the best stunt aerobatic planes are bi-planes – they look old-fashioned, but they can twist and turn like no other planes. The American Wright brothers were the first to make a successful powered flight, in 1903.

Fuselage

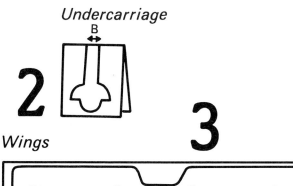

Undercarriage

Wings

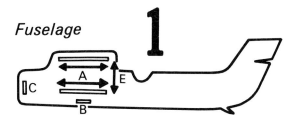

Tail Wing

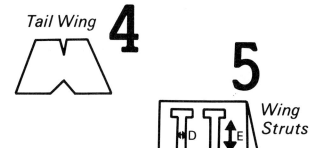

Wing Struts

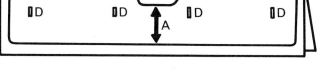

Propeller

Construction

1.
Cut out the fuselage. Make two slits, as shown (both **A**), with a small **B** slit beneath. Make a small **C** slit at the front. Make a cut into the back edge of the tailplane.

2.
Fold a piece of card in half. Draw a wheel, so that the leg width (**B**), is the same width as slit **B**. Cut out the undercarriage through both layers, but don't cut along the crease.

3.
Fold a long piece of card in half. Draw the shape of the wings, so that distance **A** is the same length as the **A** slits. Cut four small **D** slits. Cut out the wings through both layers to make an identical pair of wings.

4.
Cut out the tail wing. Make a cut in from the front edge.

5.
Fold a piece of card in half. Draw two struts as wide as the **D** slits, and as long as distance **E** (see Step **1**), the distance between the **A** slits. Make T-shape endings at the top and bottom. Cut them both out through both layers to make four identical struts.

6.
Fold a piece of card in half. Draw a propeller blade, then cut it out through both layers to make two identical blades.

A

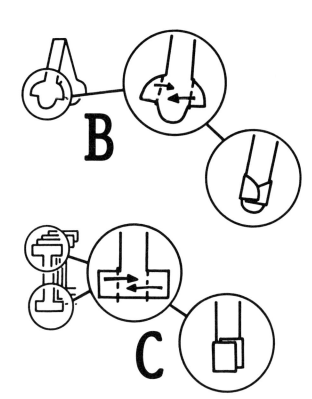

B

C

D

Assembly

A.
Fold in the wider trailing edge of one half of both wings.

B.
Make two folds at the end of one wheel.

C.
Fold in the tabs at the ends of all four struts.

D.
*Push the folded section of each wing through an **A** slit, then unfold the wings. Push the undercarriage through the **B** slit and fold it in the middle. Unfold the end. Slot on the tail wing.*

E.
*Push the ends of each strut through a pair of **D** slits, opening out the T-shapes to lock the struts to the wings. Push the propeller blades through the **C** slit.*

F.
The Bi-plane complete. Hang it from three threads (see 'How to Suspend a Model').

G.
Using the same technique to lock the struts to the wings, you can make this simpler mono-plane, or perhaps a complicated tri-plane – a plane with three wings!

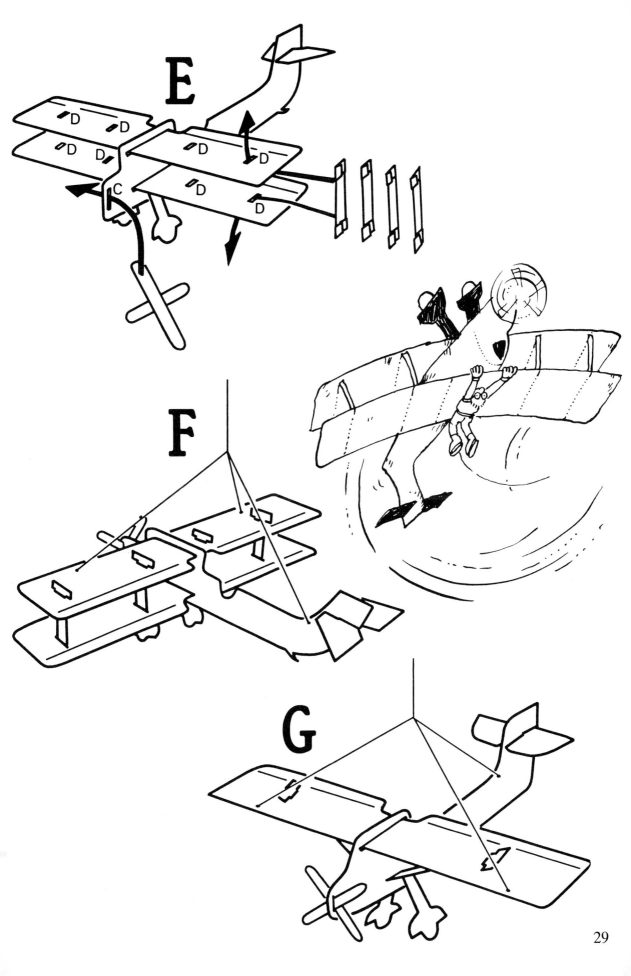

E

F

G

29

Kite

Why is a kite called a kite? Because the first kites looked like the kite bird. Kites were flown by the ancient Chinese as a pastime and even by New Zealand Maoris as part of their religious ceremonies. Today there are many different designs, some very bizarre. Why not invent your own for a special kite mobile?

Construction

1.
Cut out the shape of the kite. Make a small slit across the bottom at **A**.

2.
On a sheet of card, draw out a number of interlocking bow shapes. Measure **B**, the narrowest part of each bow.

3.
Cut out a long tail as wide as slit **A**, with a T-shape at one end. Make a series of **B** slits the same width as **B** measured in Step **2.**

4.
Make two creases on the kite, so that ...

5.
... when unfolded, the edges of the kite curve inwards and the centre point rises up (or dips away, if you are looking at the card from the other side!).

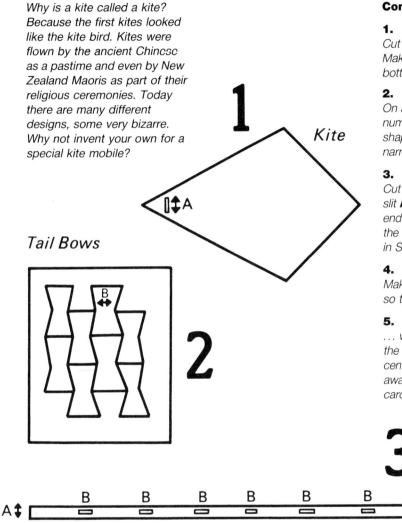

Kite

Tail Bows

Tail

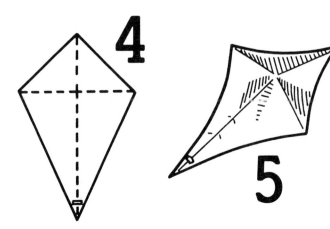

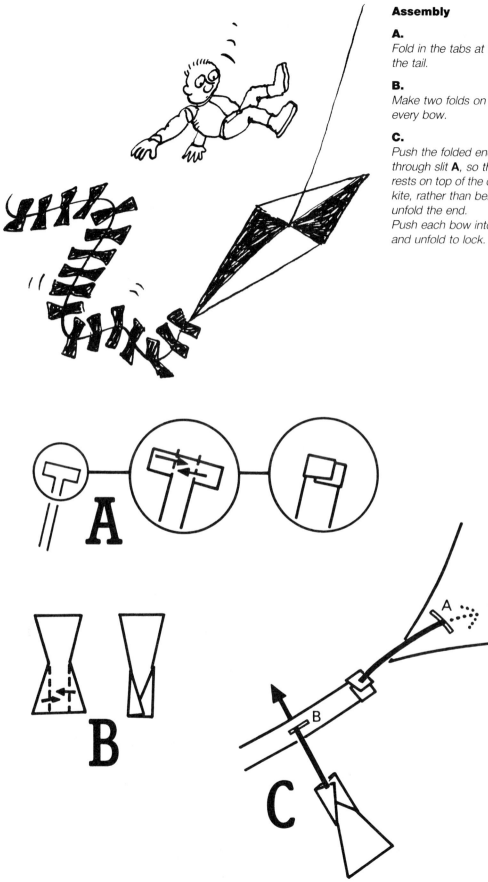

Assembly

A.

Fold in the tabs at the T end of the tail.

B.

Make two folds on one side of every bow.

C.

*Push the folded end of the tail through slit **A**, so that the tail rests on top of the corner of the kite, rather than below it, and unfold the end.*
*Push each bow into its **B** slit and unfold to lock.*

D.
The Kite complete. Hang it from three threads (see 'How to Suspend a Model').

Balloon

Balloons were the first craft invented to carry people up into the skies, way back in the 1700s. In recent years, specially designed balloons have carried people huge distances across the Atlantic and Pacific oceans and up to almost the very top of the atmosphere. Balloons have a practical use too, in taking weather-forecasting instruments and cameras into the sky.

Construction

1.

Fold a piece of card in half. Using a pair of compasses or something circular like a jamjar lid, cup or roll of tape, draw a circle. Draw the neck of the balloon on the circle. Cut out the shape through both layers to make two identical balloon shapes.

2.
Carefully draw five squares in a + shape. To each of them, add a tab as shown. Cut out the shape very carefully.

3.
On one balloon shape (X) make slit **A**, as shown.

4.
On the other shape (Y), make two cuts, so that the gap between them is the same length as slit **A**.

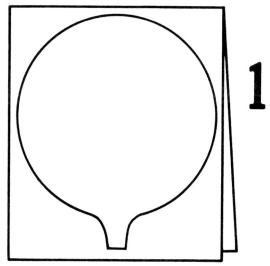

Balloon

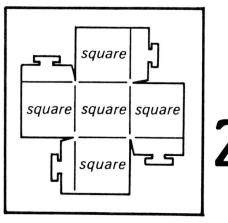

Basket

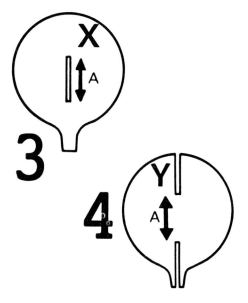

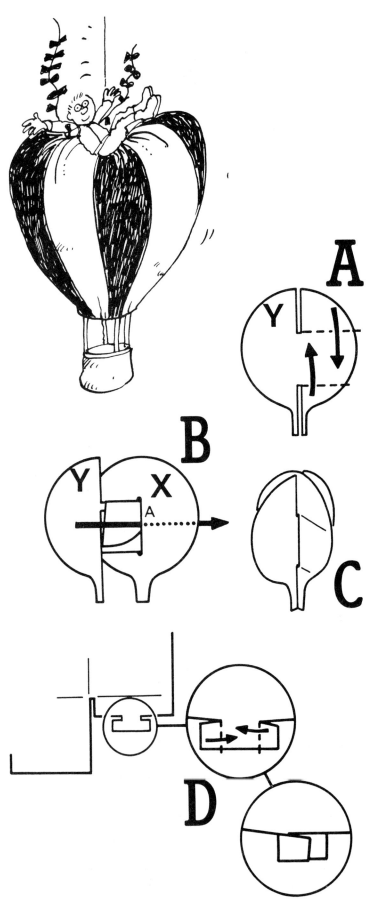

Assembly

A.
Make two folds in Y, as shown.

B.
Push the folded section through the **A** slit and unfold.

C.
The Balloon complete.

D.
On the basket, fold in the tabs on all four sides in preparation for a Bar Lock.

E.
Crease where shown along the dotted lines to fold the card into a basket shape.

F.
Make pencil dots where the tabs were folded in, then make a slit between the dots.

G.
Push each tab through its slit. Unfold the tabs inside the basket to lock them tight.

H.
The basket complete.

I.
To hang the basket from the balloon, thread a needle with a long length of cotton. Push the needle through a corner of the basket, then up through the widest part of the balloon, back down through the next corner, up through the next widest part of the balloon, and so on until the zig-zag of threading is complete. Adjust the thread so that the basket hangs level beneath the balloon and tie the ends of the thread together. Suspend the balloon from a single thread.

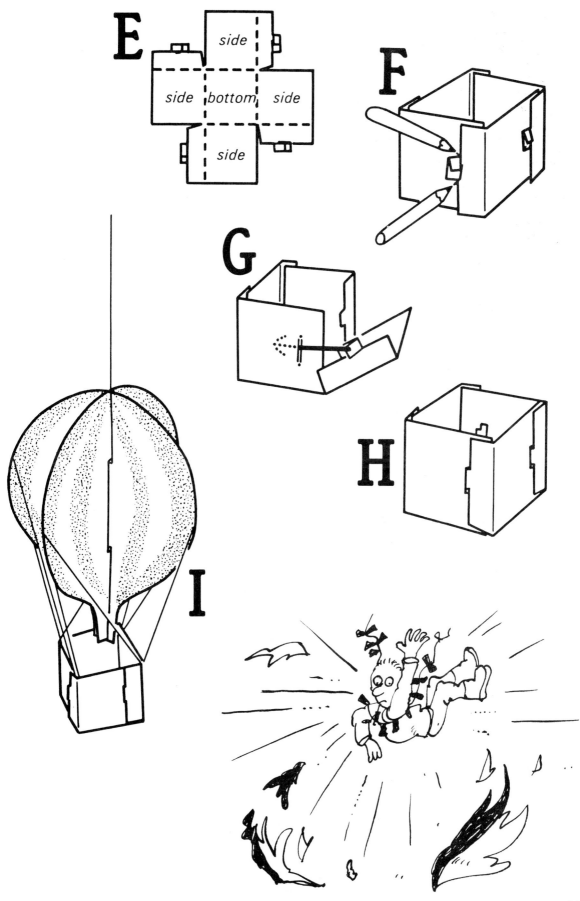

E

side

side bottom side

side

F

G

H

I

35

Hang Glider

The earliest man-carrying hang gliders were built by the German Otto Lillienthal in the 1890s. He made some 2,500 flights and created designs that the pioneer aircraft builders would later follow. Hang gliding became popular in the 1970s and today many people enjoy the thrill of soaring around the sky like a bird.

Construction

1.
Fold a piece of card in half. Draw the shape of a wing. Make a small slit at **A**, through both layers. Cut out the wing through both layers, without cutting along the fold.

2.
Cut out the pilot. Make a small slit at **B**.

3.
Fold a piece of card in half. Draw an arm, sloping to the left, as shown, which is as wide as slit **B**. Cut it out through both layers. Add a small cut to the front edge of each wrist, as shown.

4.
Cut out the bar as shown, as wide as slit **A** and with a T-shape at each end. Fold the ends upwards, and make two cuts in the middle section of the bar, one near each crease.

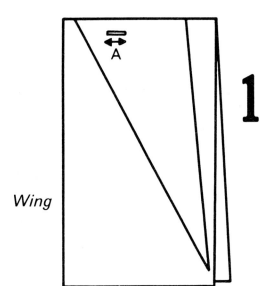

Wing

1

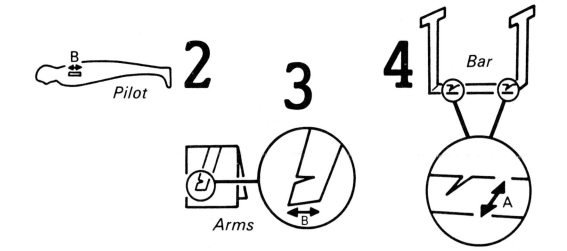

Pilot **2**

3 Arms

4 Bar

Assembly

A.
Push the arms through slit **B** in the pilot.

B.
Fold in the tabs at each end of the bar.

C.
Slot the wrists into the bar. The arms should make an upside-down V-shape when locked to the bar. If they do not, make some more (easy!) and adjust the placement of the cuts.

D.
Push the folded ends of the bar through the **A** slits. Unfold the ends to lock the bar to the wing.

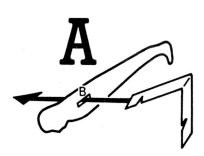

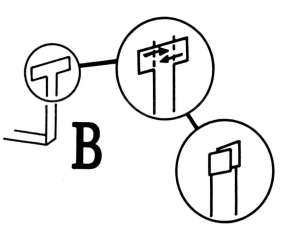

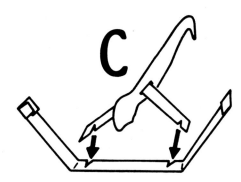

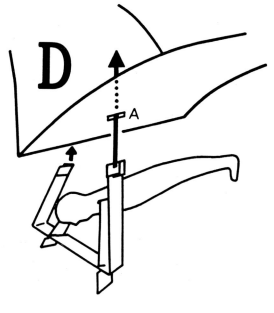

E.

Curl the wings gently between your fingers. The Hang Glider is now complete. Hang it from three threads (see 'How to Suspend a Model').

F.

Hang Glider wings come in many shapes. Add some variety to your mobile by making hang gliders with wings shaped like these, or invent your own.

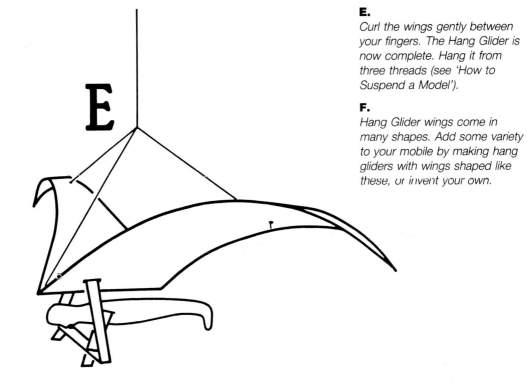

Bird

Some birds have amazing eyesight. A bird of prey, for example, can see another bird 5 miles (8 km) away. The largest bird that can fly is the albatross – it has a huge 12-ft (3.60 m) wingspan. The smallest is the hummingbird, which is only 2¼ in (5.7 cm) long. Some scientists believe that birds are descended from small dinosaurs.

Construction

1.
*Cut out the body. Make a long slit **A** and a shorter slit **B** beneath it. Make a cut in the back edge of the tail. Cut out an eye (or make eyes like the ones in the Man in the Moon.*

2.
Cut out a tail. Make a cut in the centre front.

3.
*Fold a piece of card in half. Measure slit **A** and mark the same length on the crease. Draw a wing as wide as **A**. Cut it out through both layers, but don't cut along the crease.*

4.
*Fold a piece of card in half. Draw a leg sloping forward, as wide as slit **B**. Cut it out through both layers, but not along the crease.*

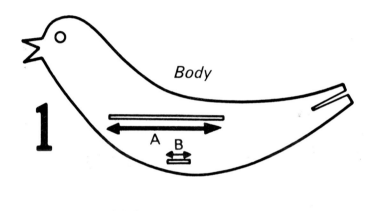

Body

A B

1

Tail

2

A

Wings

3

Legs   B

4

Assembly

A.

Fold in the sides of a foot.

B.

*Push the folded foot through slit **B**. Push the wings through slit **A**. Slot on the tail.*

C.

The Bird complete. Hang it from three threads (see 'How to Suspend a Model').

D.

Birds, of course, come in many shapes and sizes. Try making this seagull, or perhaps something more exotic like a hummingbird. Look in books about birds for ideas.

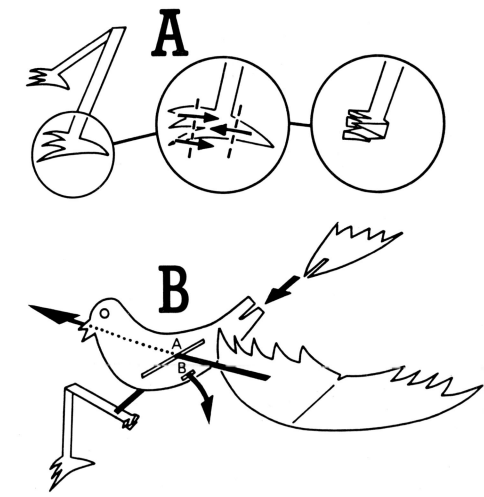

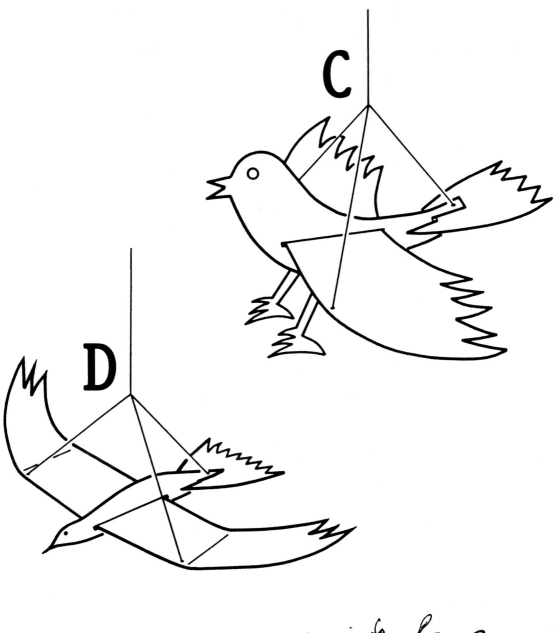

C

D

Butterfly

Unexpectedly, butterflies have probably the most acute sense of smell of all creatures. Some butterflies can smell others of the same species an incredible 7 miles (11 km) away. Even stranger, many butterflies are iridescent – that is, they change colour depending on the angle from which they are seen, rather like a pool of petrol.

Construction

1.
Fold a piece of card in half. Draw the shape of a hind wing (curved) and a fore wing (more pointed). Cut them out through both layers, but don't cut along the crease.

2.
Cut out a body. Make a long slit **A** and a short slit **B**.

3.
Fold a piece of card in half. Draw an antenna so that the part touching the crease is the same width as slit **B**. Cut it out through both layers.

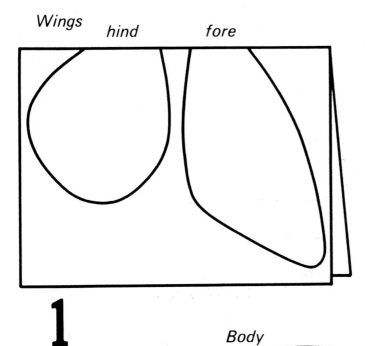

Wings   *hind*   *fore*

1

Body

2

3

Antennae

Assembly

A.
Fold in the end of one antenna.

B.
Fold in one fore wing, as shown.

C.
Fold in one hind wing.

D.
*Push both the folded wings through slit **A** and push the folded antenna through slit **B**. Unfold everything.*

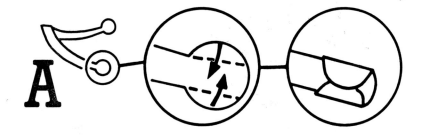

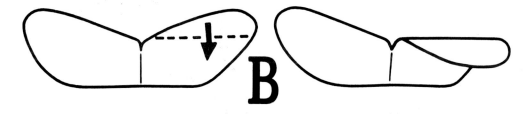

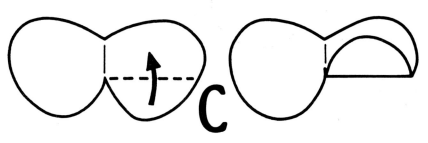

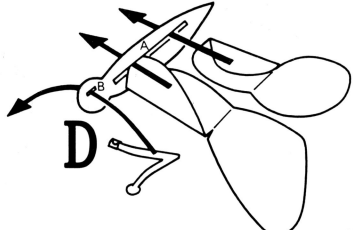

E.

The Butterfly complete. Hang it from three threads (see 'How to Suspend a Model').

F.

Using the same techniques as before, make these exotic types of African butterfly. Cut the wings out very carefully and colour them with bold patterns.

E

F

Bat

Bats are not birds (birds have feathers and lay eggs) but mammals (which have fur and give birth to live young), and they are the only mammals which can fly. They have a remarkable inbuilt radar which lets them fly in complete darkness without hitting anything.

Construction

1.
Fold a piece of card in half. Draw a wing, then cut it out through both layers, but don't cut along the fold.

2.
Cut out the body. Make slit **A**. Make a cut in the back edge. Cut out the eye.

3.
Fold a piece of card in half. Measure slit **A** and mark the same length on the crease. Draw an ear as wide as **A**. Cut it out through both layers.

4.
Unfold the wings and make a cut in the centre of the front edge. Make creases where shown to give the wings some shape.

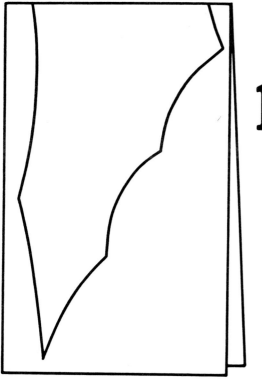

Wings

Body

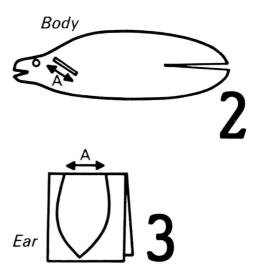

Ear

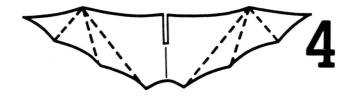

Assembly

A.
Fold in part of an ear, as shown.

B.
Push the folded ear through slit **A**. *Unfold it to lock the ear to the body. Slot on the wings.*

C.
The Bat complete. Hang it from three threads (see 'How to Suspend a Model').

C

ANGUS & ROBERTSON PUBLISHERS

*Unit 4, Eden Park, 31 Waterloo Road,
North Ryde, NSW, Australia 2113, and
16 Golden Square, London W1R 4BN,
United Kingdom*

*First published in the United Kingdom
by Angus & Robertson (UK) in 1989.
First published in Australia by
Angus & Robertson Publishers in 1989.*

*Copyright © Paul Jackson 1989
Illustrations copyright © Scoular Anderson 1989*

*British Library Cataloguing in Publication Data
Jackson, Paul.
  Flying mobiles
  1. Mobiles. Making – Manuals – For children
  I. Title
  731'.55*

ISBN 0 207 16173 9

Typeset by New Faces, Bedford

*Printed in Great Britain by Scotprint Ltd,
Musselburgh, Scotland*